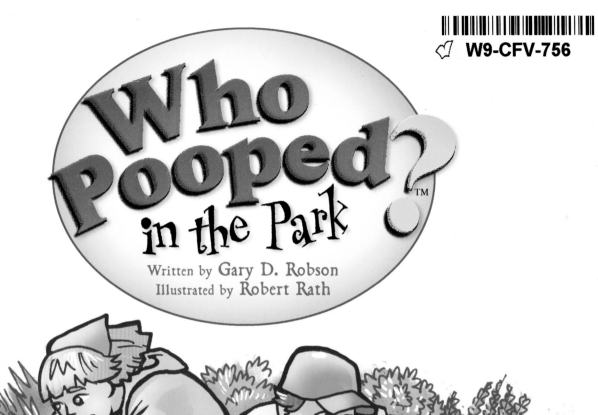

Who Pooped in the Park?™

Written by Gary D. Robson

Illustrated by Robert Rath

FARCOUNTRY
PRESS

Thanks to Wanda Moran at Acadia National Park
for her help with this book.
- Gary

For Lucy and Thomas, my poop experts.
- Robert

ISBN 13: 978-1-56037-338-4
ISBN 10: 1-56037-338-5

© 2006 Farcountry Press
Text © 2006 Gary D. Robson
Illustrations © 2006 Farcountry Press

Who Pooped in the Park? is a registered trademark of Farcountry Press.

Manufactured by
Everbest Printing
334 Huanshi Road South
Dachong Western Industrial District
Panyu, Guangdong, China
in May 2013
Printed in China.

For more information on our books,
write Farcountry Press, P.O. Box 5630, Helena, MT 59604;
call (800) 821-3874; or visit www.farcountrypress.com.

Book design by Robert Rath.
Created, produced, and designed in the United States.

17 16 15 14 13   2 3 4 5 6

Library of Congress Cataloging-in-Publication Data

Robson, Gary D.
   Who pooped in the park?. Acadia National Park / [Gary D. Robson, Robert Rath].
      p. cm.
   ISBN-13: 978-1-56037-338-4
   1. Animal tracks--Maine--Acadia National Park--Juvenile literature. I. Rath, Robert. II. Title.
   QL768.R613 2006
   591.9741'45--dc22

                     2005016252

"Dad? I have to go to the bathroom."
Michael squirmed in the back seat.

"We'll be at our campground in just
a little while," said Dad. "We're in
Acadia National Park now."

"He's just nervous," said Michael's sister. "He thinks
a bear's gonna eat him." She growled at Michael
and made her fingers look like claws.

"Stop it, Emily," said Mom. "Nobody
is getting eaten by anything."

Michael was very excited about the trip, but Emily was right. He *was* nervous.

He had just read a book about grizzly bears. He knew how big they could get.

And he was afraid that a hungry bear would eat just about anything—maybe even a boy.

"I *am* kind of scared of grizzly bears," admitted Michael.

"Don't worry," Dad told him. "There are no grizzlies around here. Just a few black bears."

Mom reached back and held Michael's hand. She said, "We'll show you how to count a black bear's toes and never get close enough to be scared."

"Here's our campsite. Let's set up the tent. Then we can go for a walk and we'll show you what we mean," Dad said.

Michael was pretty worried about bear toes, but tried not to show it.

"Let's hurry!" said Emily. "I want to see some animals!"

Once the tent was up, the whole family went for a hike.

Emily started to complain before they even left the campground. "I haven't seen any animals yet. Maybe there aren't any here!"

"Sure there are," said Dad. "Let's see what we can learn about them from their *sign*."

"Sign?" said Michael. "You mean like a sign at the zoo?"

GREAT HORNED OWL

WHITE-TAILED DEER

PORCUPINE

Dad chuckled. "In this case," he replied, "a sign is a clue that an animal has left behind."

"See where all the bark was stripped off of that tree?" added Mom. "That's a sign of a porcupine having his lunch."

Dad said, "Look around the base of the tree and I'll bet we'll find more sign."

the STRAIGHT POOP

Porcupines love to eat bark. Sometimes they'll climb a tree and eat the bark all the way around, killing the tree.

Michael was starting to get excited. "Look! There are footprints here!"

"Yes," said Mom. "Those are porcupine tracks. See the marks where it dragged its tail?"

the STRAIGHT
POOP

Porcupines can't throw their quills, as some people believe. The quills are very sharp, so it's best to leave porcupines alone.

"And there's porcupine scat over here," said Dad.

"*Scat*?" asked Emily, looking a little less grumpy. "What's *scat*?"

"It's the word hikers and trackers use for animal poop," Dad replied.

"See, Michael," said Dad. "We don't have to get up close to an animal to learn about it. Instead of a close encounter of the *scary* kind, we'll have a close encounter of the *poopy* kind."

Everybody laughed, and Mom made a gross-out face.

"Dad! Mom! Look over here! I found bunny scat!" yelled Michael. "It's just like what we have in Fluffy's cage."

"We came all the way to Acadia National Park for *that*?" grumbled Emily. "Michael's bunny makes plenty of poop at home."

the STRAIGHT POOP

Rabbits and hares eat their own scat! They do this to get as much nutrition from the food as they can. The little brown balls are scat that's already been through twice.

Dad said, "Around here, it's probably from a hare rather than a rabbit."

"A hare?" asked Emily.

"They're like rabbits, only bigger," answered Dad. "They usually have longer back legs and bigger feet, too. See these tracks?"

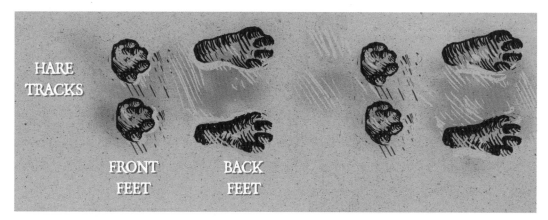

HARE TRACKS

FRONT FEET   BACK FEET

"Yes, it's a snowshoe hare," said Mom. "See it over there?"

While everybody else looked at the hare, Michael was more interested in the scat.

"I found some even bigger bunny poop here," he announced.

"Actually, this scat is from a deer, not a rabbit or hare," Mom told him. "You can tell by the shape. Hare poop is almost round, but deer scat is shaped more like jellybeans."

the STRAIGHT POOP

Deer scat looks different in the spring because deer eat more fresh green plants then.

DEER SCAT: SPRING / SUMMER

DEER SCAT: FALL / WINTER

RABBIT SCAT

JELLYBEANS

Michael found some marks in the dirt. "Are these deer tracks?" he asked.

"Yes!" said Mom. "They're from a white-tailed deer. See how they're split? Deer hooves have two parts."

"What are these little marks?" asked Emily. She was starting to get interested.

the STRAIGHT POOP

Moose tracks look a lot like deer tracks, but they're more round and much larger.

DEW CLAW

"Those are from its dew claws," said Mom. "They're little claws behind the hoof. Dew claws sometimes show in deer tracks in soft ground. Lots of other animals have dew claws, too, including cats and dogs."

"Oh, no!" said Michael. "Here's one
of its antlers! Did a bear eat the deer?"
Michael looked around nervously.

Dad bent down by the antler.
"This deer didn't get eaten. Its antler fell off.
Deer shed their antlers every winter
and then grow a new, bigger set
the next year."

the STRAIGHT POOP

Female deer, elk, and moose
don't grow antlers. Caribou
are the only members of the
deer family in which both males
and females have antlers.

"This deer was in a hurry, though," said Mom, as she studied the ground.

Michael and Emily went over to look.

"How can you tell?" said Emily. She was having fun finding all the clues the animals left behind.

"The hoofprints get very far apart here," Mom explained, "and the back prints are in front of the front prints."

"It was walking backwards?" said Emily.

"No, it was galloping. Something scared it and it was moving fast." Mom said.

BACK HOOVES

FRONT HOOVES

WALKING · GALLOPING

GALLOPING

"Here's what scared the deer,"
Dad said. "There are coyote tracks
and scat all around here."

"Some of the tracks are small,
like they're from pups," said Mom.
"I'll bet their den is nearby."

the STRAIGHT POOP

Don't go looking for coyote dens! Mother animals get very protective around their babies.

the STRAIGHT POOP

One way to tell coyote scat from dog scat is by the hair and bits of bones in the coyote scat.

"These coyote tracks look like dog tracks," said Emily.

"That's because the coyote is a member of the dog family," explained Mom.

"Coyote scat looks like dog poop, too," Michael said, "but it's got a bunch of other stuff in it."

"That's hair and bones from the animals it's been eating," Dad explained.

the STRAIGHT POOP

Coyotes eat just about anything they can catch, and steal leftovers from other predators, too.

25

Michael had forgotten all about being scared of bears. A little farther down the trail, he spotted some more tracks.

"Here are some smaller coyote tracks," he said. "Are they from a pup?"

the STRAIGHT POOP

Both red fox scat and coyote scat can have berries, insects, and plant parts in it, along with bits of bone and fur. Red fox scat is much smaller than coyote scat.

COYOTE

RED FOX

"They might be," Mom said, "but I think they're from a red fox. They're very common around here, and this scat has berries in it."

27

"Hey, look!" said Emily.
"Let's go down by the stream."

"Okay," said Mom, "but be careful, kids.
Don't get too close to the water."

"There are tracks here, too,"
said Michael.

"Tracks show up really well in
muddy or wet ground," said Dad.
"These are webbed tracks. Can you
guess what they're from?"

"Ducks?" said Emily.

"Not ducks…," teased Mom.

"...river otters!" she finished. "See them playing across the stream?"

the STRAIGHT POOP

Because otters catch and eat fish, their scat smells "fishy" and usually has scales and fish bones in it.

"You can find lots of tracks by the stream," said Dad. "Raccoons like to hang out here, too."

"Let's head up the trail toward those rocks," Mom suggested. "I think we might see something new up there."

RACCOON
TRACK

PORCUPINE
TRACK

OTTER
TRACK

Sure enough, the kids spotted something interesting when they reached the rocks.

"What are these white streaks on the rocks over here?" he asked.

"That's called guano," said Dad.

the STRAIGHT POOP

Guano makes very good fertilizer. People buy bags of it to spread in their gardens to keep their plants healthy.

"I know what that is!" exclaimed Emily.
"We learned about it in school.
Guano is bat poop!"

"Right," said Mom. "There are
a lot of different bats in
Acadia National Park.
The most common is
the little brown bat."

"Do they suck blood like vampires?" said Michael with a shudder.

"Oh no, they're just tiny bats that eat bugs," said Mom with a smile. "There are no vampire bats around here."

the STRAIGHT POOP

Bats sleep hanging upside-down and like to perch in caves, trees, and holes in the rock.

35

the STRAIGHT POOP

Each owl foot has four toes, usually with two toes pointing forward and two pointing backward. Owls can shift their toes so that they have three pointing forward and one backward.

Emily noticed something strange on the tree.

"Is this more bat poop?" she asked.

"That poop is from an owl," Dad said. He looked down at the ground below the tree and added, "See these tracks with three toes pointing forward and one pointing back, and the owl pellets around the base of the tree?"

"Owl pellets?" said Emily.

"Owls eat their prey whole," explained Dad. "The parts they can't digest, like hair and bones, get coughed up in a pellet like this."

the STRAIGHT POOP

Studying owl pellets is a great way to find out what owls eat. Great horned owls dine on a wide variety of small animals, including snakes, rabbits, porcupines, and birds — even other types of owls!

"Yuck!" said the kids.

"Those tracks and pellets are really big," said Michael. "Are they from a big owl?"

"You can tell the size of an owl from its tracks and pellets," answered Mom. "These are probably from a great horned owl. They're some of the biggest owls in Acadia National Park."

the STRAIGHT POOP

Owls see very well at night, but they aren't blind during the day, like some people believe. They see just fine then, too.

"Whoa! Why is all of the bark torn off this tree?" Michael asked. "Did another porcupine do that?"

"This is different," replied Mom. "An animal was sharpening its claws on this tree, not eating the bark."

"And if you look how high those scratch marks go, it was pretty big!" added Mom.

"It's not just the animal that's big," said Emily. "Look at the size of this poop!"

"It looks like we found your black bear," said Mom. "Let's see what you learned today. What can you figure out about this bear?"

"It must be as tall as you, and it has really long claws," said Michael.

"It's been eating plants," said Emily, "because there's no hair or bones in this poop."

"Good job!" Mom said. "What else?"

the STRAIGHT POOP

Black bears eat almost anything. They mostly dine on leaves, nuts, berries, insects, twigs, and honey, but they also hunt small animals and fish.

"Here's the bear's footprint," said Michael. "It's really big, and it has more toes than a coyote or mountain lion."

"I told you you'd be able to count a black bear's toes," laughed Dad.

"It rubbed off some hair on the tree," said Emily. "You said this was a black bear, but these hairs are reddish brown."

"Black bears can be all different colors," explained Mom. "They can be black, brown, or cinnamon-colored, like this one. There are even black bears that are almost white."

As the family ate dinner that night, everyone talked about how much fun they had.

"We didn't see very many animals," said Emily, "but it seemed like we did!"

44

Everyone laughed when Michael said, "And I didn't get scared once!"

TRACKS and

BLACK BEAR

Tracks are large with five visible toes and claws.

Scat changes depending on diet but usually contains vegetation.

RACCOON

Tracks are large for the animal's size. Five bulbous toes.

Scat is blunt on ends, and may contain dangerous parasites.

DON'T TOUCH RACCOON SCAT!

RIVER OTTER

Tracks are similar to raccoon tracks, but feet are webbed.

Scat usually has fish scales and bones in it.

SNOWSHOE HARE

Tracks are filled in and it's hard to see details because feet are full of fur.

Scat is small and round.

EASTERN CHIPMUNK

Four toes on front track and five on back.

Scat is tiny, long ovals, much smaller than snowshoe hare.

SCAT NOTES

COYOTE

Tracks are like a dog's, with four toes, usually with visible claw marks.

Scat is very dark colored with tapered ends and usually contains hair.

RED FOX

Tracks are smaller than a coyote's, with a ridge on the large pad.

Scat is similar to coyote, but often contains plant and insect parts.

WHITE-TAILED DEER

Tracks show a pointed split hoof.

Scat is oval-shaped like jellybeans.

LITTLE BROWN BAT

Bats rarely land on soft ground to leave tracks.

Scat is runny and white.

GREAT HORNED OWL

Tracks show four toes: two pointing forward and two backward or sideways.

Scat is runny and white. "Cough pellets" contain fur and bones.

ABOUT the AUTHOR and ILLUSTRATOR

GARY ROBSON lives in Montana near Yellowstone National Park, where he and his wife own a bookstore and tea bar. Gary has written dozens of books and hundreds of articles, mostly related to science, nature, and technology.
www.robson.org/gary

ROBERT RATH is a book designer and illustrator living in Bozeman, Montana. Although he has worked with Scholastic Books, Lucasfilm, and Montana State University, his favorite project is keeping up with his family.

BOOKS IN THE WHO POOPED IN THE PARK?™ SERIES:

Acadia National Park
Big Bend National Park
Black Hills
Cascades
Colorado Plateau
Death Valley National Park
Glacier National Park
Grand Canyon National Park
Grand Teton National Park
Great Smoky Mountains National Park
Northwoods
Olympic National Park
Red Rock Canyon National Conservation Area
Rocky Mountain National Park
Sequoia and Kings Canyon National Parks
Shenandoah National Park
Sonoran Desert
Yellowstone National Park
Yosemite National Park